A restored paddle wheel steamer gracefully plys the Murray River in Victoria. In bygone days, these craft were the main form of transport in the Murray Valley.

Friendly lorikeets at Currumbin Bird Sanctuary at Currumbin on the Gold Coast.

AUSTRALIA

The waratah (see page 9).

Text by Dalys Newman

NATIONAL
BOOK DISTRIBUTORS AND PUBLISHERS

Wildflowers in Western Australia (see page 33).
Front cover: The koala (see page 37).
Back cover: The kangaroo (see page 43).

Published by National Book Distributors and Publishers
3/2 Aquatic Drive, Frenchs Forest, NSW 2086
First published in 1988 as *Dinkum Aussie Picture Book*
Second edition (paperback) 1989
Reprinted 1989, 1991, 1993, 1994, 1996
Text and captions by Dalys Newman
All photographs except cover © Australian Picture Library, 1988, 1989
Cover photograph: Christine Mulcahy
Printed in Singapore by Kyodo Printing Co (S'pore) Pte Ltd
Typesetting processed by Deblaere Typesetting Pty Ltd

National Library of Australia
Cataloguing-in-Publication data
Newman, Dalys.
    [Dinkum Aussie picture book]. Australia.

Includes index.
ISBN 1 875580 38 7.

1. Australia — Description and travel — 1976–1990 — Views.
2. Australia — Social life and customs — 1976–1990 — Pictorial works.
I. Australian Picture Library. II. Title. III. Title: Dinkum Aussie picture book

994.0630222

INTRODUCTION

Australia is different. She is both the youngest and oldest of continents: the oldest geologically and the youngest in development.

Australia was the last great habitable area to be surveyed and colonised by Europeans. It was only two hundred years ago—26 January 1788—when Captain Arthur Phillip, first Governor of the colony, along with some 1487 convicts, civilians and soldiers, landed at Sydney Cove to establish a precarious toehold on this unique continent. These First Fleeters had the unenviable task of settling the new, unknown land. What queer and alarming discoveries they must have made: extraordinary animals that ran, jumped, leapt and vol-

planed like none they had seen before; baby animals that found refuge in a pouch on their mother's abdomen; strange furry creatures that lived in rivers and laid eggs like birds; and there were trees that shed their bark instead of leaves. No wonder the Old World thought Australia topsy-turvy when reports of these wondrous sights filtered back. These early settlers survived their struggles and the infant nation grew in strength—being transformed from a penal colony into a bright land of opportunity whose wondrous sights are now enjoyed by millions.

The ancient landmass of Australia is the world's largest island and smallest continent. Here are the oldest known fragments of the earth's crust, dated at 4.3 billion years. Australia's isolation from other lands makes her geologically and topographically unique. Nowhere else in the world will you find anything so remarkable as Ayers Rock, the biggest monolith on

Rays of sunlight set tree ferns aglow in the magnificent rainforests. Tropical, subtropical and temperate rainforests are found in high rainfall areas along the east coast and highlands from Cape York to Tasmania.

Boxing kangaroos—rearing back on their tails, they grapple and kick with long-clawed feet. These deadly claws have taken the lives of attacking dogs and men.

nificent heart of the continent. This huge plateau of arid and semi-arid land is coloured in rich reds and ochres and is only sparsely vegetated. It is generally vast, flat, featureless country where cattle stations are measured in thousands of square kilometres and fresh water is a precious commodity. Here and there mountainous ridges of cracked rock, and huge salt and mud pans break the monotony. It is the great Australian Outback—land of unparalleled and powerful beauty.

This fierce sunburnt country has forced an adherence to the coast—over 80 per cent of the population find security in urban areas on the coastal strips, separated by mountain chains from the strange wilderness beyond. Australia has increasingly become a nation of city people; almost a quarter of the 16 million population live in one city alone—Sydney. Despite the usual ravages of civilisation, these Australian cities are places of vibrant beauty—Sydney's harbour, spanned by its famous bridge and decorated with the lofty sails of the Opera House, is one of the finest in the world and a trademark of this country. And despite the Ocker image of the Australian, these cities are multicultural melting pots. Over two million immigrants from more than thirty countries have brought their history and culture to add a rich depth to this young nation.

Colourful and bustling cities contrast with the lazy, fly-buzzed, dust-streaked charm of the scattered country towns that add yet another dimension to this patchwork pattern that is Australian life. Here, time takes it easy and you can almost see the ghosts of the bushrangers, gold-diggers and pioneers of a bygone era.

Wherever any Australian lives, whatever her or his occupation or race, she or he is generally serious about the pursuit of leisure. The Great Australian Outdoors is a tourist's and sportsperson's paradise. The balmy climate and superb scenery have given rise to a nation of people who take their pleasure in the open air. Rolling surf beaches, beautiful harbours, spectacular and diverse national parks, paddlewheel steamers on the Murray, bush race meetings, opal towns where miners sleep with their .38s under their pillows, palm-thatched islands on the Great Barrier Reef ... the land has bountiful wealth for all to enjoy and explore.

For people who have not trodden Australia's shores, the land is magical and remote, a country fabled for its Outback myths, strange marsupials and people who wear hats with corks dangling from them. For Australians it is the 'lucky country', a place where everyone can find a lifestyle of one's own—whether it be in one of the populous major cities or in the solitude of the Outback.

earth, 350 metres high and 8 kilometres around the base; and the Great Barrier Reef, whose 2000 kilometre chain of vibrant corals is truly one of the wonders of the world.

Australia is a land of contrasts and contradictions: it is the driest continent on earth but in parts the average rainfall exceeds 375 centimetres; the flattest continent but its mountains, from the snow-capped peaks of south-west Tasmania to the blazing red domes of the MacDonnell Ranges in the Northern Territory, are scenically stunning. Even the Australian bush is full of contrasts: dense conifer forest, open savannah, vine-festooned jungle or barren heathland. But there is one constant in the midst of all these variables—the mag-

A ferry steadfastly chugs her way alongside the great grey arch of Sydney Harbour Bridge.

Sydney Harbour Bridge stretches across azure waters to link the North Shore to the South. Opened in 1932, the Coathanger, as it is affectionately known, is 503 metres long.

(Following pages)
Storm clouds gather over rolling wheat plains. More than a thousand new varieties of wheat have been bred to suit Australian conditions and this country is now one of the leading world exporters of wheat.

Most majestic of all Australian wildflowers—the waratah, floral emblem of New South Wales.

Music sticks and the rhythmic drone of the didjeridu (didgeridoo) provide accompaniment for many Aboriginal ceremonies and dances.

Cattle mustering—the immense cattle stations of Australia often cover more than 10 000 square kilometres in area.

Thar she blows! The spectacular blowhole at Kiama, New South Wales, shoots water up to a height of 60 metres.

(Right)
Worshipping the sun on one of Sydney's many golden beaches.

Tourists pan for gold at Sovereign Hill, a major reconstruction of a gold-mining settlement near Ballarat, Victoria.

Australia's most powerful lighthouse stands sentinel at Cape Byron, New South Wales, the most easterly point on the Australian mainland.

Salesmanship at the Ettamogah pub near Albury, New South Wales.

The peaceful Hawkesbury River at Brooklyn, New South Wales.

Sydney's most distinctive landmarks—the soaring sails of the Opera House and the splendid arch of the Harbour Bridge.

The Sydney Opera House, recognised as one of the wonders of the modern world, was designed by Danish architect Joern Utzon and opened in 1973—fourteen years after construction began.

Sydney—Australia's first city. The gleaming white sails of the Opera House dominate the foreground; behind, the tall buildings of the metropolitan skyline loom over Circular Quay.

The mysterious bulk of Ayers Rock (Uluru in the Aboriginal language, Pitjantjatjara) in Central Australia looms out of the desert to a height of 350 metres and is about 8 kilometres in circumference. It is the largest monolith in the world. As old as time itself, Uluru is the Aboriginal people's sacred dreaming place. Weirdly eroded caves containing Aboriginal paintings in ochre and charcoal are dotted around the rock's perimeter.

Thousands of limestone pinnacles rise from a windswept stretch of white sand-drifts in Nambung National Park, in Western Australia.

Holiday-makers enjoy Rottnest Island, off Perth, Western Australia. Willem de Vlamingh described this island as a 'terrestrial paradise' when he landed here in 1696.

(Left)
Aboriginal dancing at Mandorah in the Northern Territory.

The most fearsome creature of the deep—the shark. About ninety species of shark patrol Australia's waters, extending from the centres of the surrounding oceans to the coastal shallows. The practice of netting the most populated bathing beaches has reduced the incidence of shark attack—in fact more people are likely to be killed by lightning than shark attack.

19

Winter-frosted waters of this gorge swirl under a bridge near Launceston, Tasmania.

The jockey's colours are not the only ones to be noticed at the Melbourne Cup—a day of national aberration, when fashion is just as important as the winner of the race.

The sulphur-crested cockatoo, one of Australia's most famous birds. Often seen in flocks of several thousand, these handsome birds frequent a wide variety of timbered habitats.

The Big Pineapple, a 16 metre high replica of a pineapple at the Sunshine Plantation, Nambour, Queensland. From the top floor observation deck there is a fine view of the tropical fruit plantations below.

A Town Like Alice—Alice Springs, gateway to Ayers Rock, is a thriving tourist centre.

Corals and marine life cover the Barrier Reef like layers of sparkling jewels.

A willy-willy—a small spiralling dust storm—rises into the air in the Western Australian Outback.

(Left)
Silhouette of a pensive stockman.

Coral cays are dotted along the Great Barrier Reef. The reef stretches from near the coast of Western Papua to east of Gladstone on the central Queensland coast.

Lilac-laden boughs of a jacaranda tree frame Mount Warning, near Murwillumbah in the centre of the banana and sugarcane growing district in northern New South Wales.

Sailing on the Swan River, Perth. This broad, calm expanse of water, with its conveniently central location, is a popular spot for all forms of aquatic entertainment.

Rising like monstrous pink haystacks to a height of about 450 metres above the desert plain, the Olgas are situated about 320 kilometres south-west of Alice Springs.

The twenty-eight great rock domes of the Olgas in the Northern Territory are venerated by the Aborigines as Kata Tjuta, the many-headed one.

In less than two hundred years Australia has become the leader of one of the world's oldest industries—woolgrowing. Large flocks of sheep graze on the rolling downs and vast plains of the continent's inland.

Richmond Bridge, straddling the tranquil waters of Coal River in Tasmania, is Australia's oldest bridge. It was built by convicts between 1823 and 1825.

Goannas are as much a part of Australian folklore as kangaroos—one story has it that a goanna bite will reopen every seven years. Meat-eating monitor lizards, goannas can grow to a length of about 2 metres.

Queensland's Great Barrier Reef, which covers an area of more than 200 000 square kilometres, is the largest coral reef system in the world.

Rolling surf, golden sands, high-rise buildings and marinas epitomise Surfers Paradise, on the beautiful Nerang River.

(Left)
Motorbike replaces horse for this twentieth century Australian shepherd.

A four-wheel drive wallows along a flooded Outback road. The wet season transforms this usually arid area, making it extremely hazardous for travellers.

A vibrant blue crater lake at Mount Gambier, South Australia, is encircled by lush green vegetation. This area is the centre of the largest pine plantation in Australia.

The weekend barbie—an Australian institution.

(Previous pages)
Fairy penguins, the smallest of the world's penguins, are the only ones to breed in Australia. There is a colony on Phillip Island, Victoria.

Hobart, the second-oldest city in Australia, is a mellow mixture of the old and the new. Constitution Dock, once anchorage for whaling ships, now comes into international focus as the finishing place of the Sydney to Hobart yacht race.

Reef walkers enjoy the wondrous spectacle of intermingled purple, pink, yellow, red and white corals on the Great Barrier Reef.

Wildflowers form a golden carpet after heavy rains in Western Australia. This State has almost 7000 known species of wildflowers.

The forbidding facade of the old gaol at Port Arthur, Tasmania. Preserved as a scenic reserve, this is the only substantial convict ruin in Australia. Established in 1830, it held 30 000 convicts during its existence.

Spectators throng the Sydney Cricket Ground for an Australia versus England Test match.

Crocodiles—saltwater and freshwater—are disconcerting residents of the lakes, rivers and billabongs in the north of the continent in Western Australia, the Northern Territory and Queensland.

Australia's national emblem— the wattle tree— drips golden blossoms. Over 600 species of the wattle or Acacia family are indigenous to Australia.

The relaxed town of Darwin in the Northern Territory has been largely rebuilt since struck by Cyclone Tracy in 1974.

Performing dolphins at Seaworld, a fun park on the Gold Coast. Helicopter and speedboat rides, water-ski ballet, a paddle-wheel steamer and many fun rides can be enjoyed at this entertainment complex.

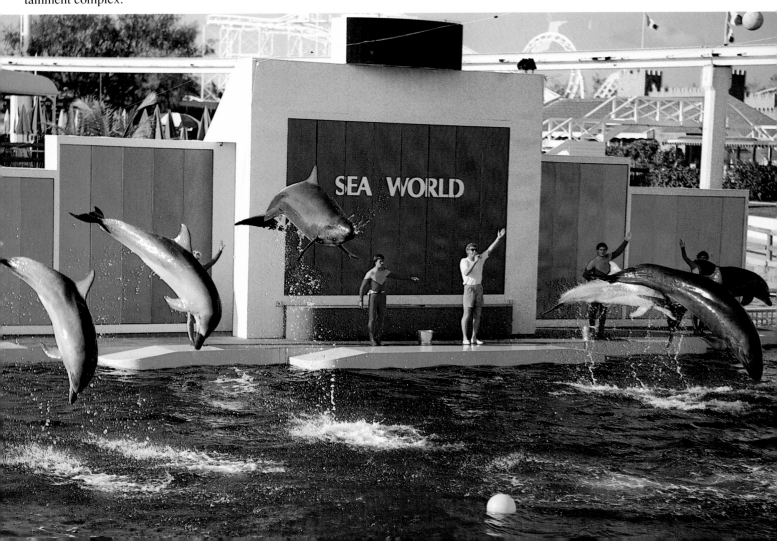

Surf-lifesaving is very much a part of the Australian way of life. Big surf carnivals attract as many as 2500 competitors and stage about 60 different events.

A surfboat full of bronzed lifesavers crashes through the rolling waves during a surf carnival. The first surf championships were held at Bondi in 1915.

(Right)

Gentle, placid and slow-moving, the koala is one of the oldest inhabitants of Australia. Its diet consists of gum leaves and the baby koala is carried in its mother's pouch for six months before emerging to ride on her back.

More than 600 species of gum trees (eucalypts) exist in Australia. They have adapted to all environments, from seashore to mountain top.

The colours of the desert: rusty reds and blues, broken only by the bleached greens of the sparse vegetation.

Lord Howe Island—a nature lover's paradise 630 kilometres north-east of Sydney. The reefs surrounding the island are frequented by more than 200 species of fish.

Las Vegas comes to Queensland—Jupiters Casino and Hotel, one of Australia's more recent tourist attractions.

Cradle Mountain mirrored in the serene waters of Lake St Clair in Tasmania.

Sugarcane fields are a common sight in Queensland. The sugar belt extends from Mossman, Queensland, to the Richmond River, New South Wales.

A mass of sail heralds the start of the Sydney to Hobart yacht race, held annually on Boxing Day (26 December). This 680 nautical mile international 'deepwater classic' is one of the world's toughest yacht races.

Clouds scud over man-made Lake Pedder in Tasmania. Part of the Hydro-Electricity Commission's giant Gordon River power development, this lake is liberally stocked with trout and is a popular tourist attraction.

An opal miner at Coober Pedy in the heart of South Australia's Outback. Anyone can try their luck after obtaining a permit from the Mines Department in Adelaide.

Broken mountains, vast plains and constantly flowing rivers make up the fascinating wilderness area of Arnhem Land, an 8 million hectare Aboriginal reserve to the east of Darwin.

Kangaroos are the best known and largest of Australian mammals. When travelling at high speed their long, heavy tails serve to keep their balance.

Wind ruffles the sand in constantly shifting patterns in the Simpson Desert.

Subtropical Brisbane—the city lights and Captain Cook Bridge are reflected in the Brisbane River which lazily wanders through this sprawling city.

Weird rock formations, shaped like prehistoric monsters, are features of the wild and majestic Kangaroo Island, off the coast of South Australia.

Rising in peaks of 1000 metres, the lofty ranges of the Grampians form the western extremity of the Great Dividing Range.

The spectacular Captain Cook Memorial Jet, set in the Central Basin of Lake Burley Griffin in Canberra. A 137 metre column of water shoots into the air, spraying a fine mist over the lake.

Branded with zinc cream. Going to the beach is almost a religious ritual for vast numbers of Australians, but today there is a greater awareness of the need for protection against the sun's harmful rays.

Incredibly rich silver-lead-zinc mines of the Barrier Range surround Broken Hill in far western New South Wales. This artificial oasis of a town, surrounded by wastelands, was created to serve the miners of the area.

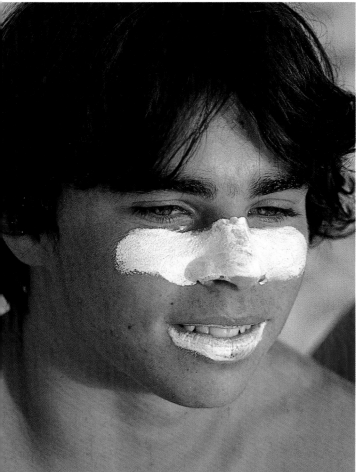

A surfer's fantasy—the remarkable 15 metre high Wave Rock in Hyden, Western Australia. Multicoloured water stains streak the surface of this bizarre granite rock which is estimated to be 2700 million years old.

A tapestry of marine paving—the unique Tessellated Pavement at Eaglehawk Neck, Tasmania.

Centred on the north bank of the Yarra River, Melbourne is Australia's second-largest city. A place of unruffled elegance, the city was founded in 1835.

(Right)
A wealth of dramatic Aboriginal art adorns Nourlangie Rock in Kakadu National Park in the Northern Territory.

A charming homestead graces a vineyard in the Barossa Valley,
South Australia, Australia's premier wine-producing area.

Pink Lake, a dense saltwater lake near Esperance, Western
Australia.

(Right)
The jagged rock monoliths of the Twelve Apostles stand fast in
swirling seas to guard the foreshore of the Port Campbell National
Park, Victoria.

Tranquil water, home of stringrays, sharks and sawfish, flows between the colourful walls of Geikie Gorge in the Kimberleys, Western Australia. The change of colour in the rock face marks the high-water mark in the wet season.

The Three Sisters look out over the hazy cliffs and valleys of the Blue Mountains National Park. This extraordinary rock formation is at Echo Point, near Katoomba, New South Wales.

Sunbathers enjoy the golden sands at Australia's most famous playground—Surfers Paradise.

Sydney Harbour is a sparkling paradise for anything that floats. Today, thousands of pleasure craft now enjoy what Captain Arthur Phillip, first Governor of New South Wales, described in 1788 as 'the finest harbour in the world, in which a thousand ships of the line may ride in the most perfect security'.

Dramatic limestone cliffs fringe the treeless, flat-topped Nullarbor plateau which extends parallel with the Great Australian Bight for about 550 kilometres and inland to a depth of about 250 kilometres.

(Following pages)
Stunted vegetation dots the vast Nullarbor Plain. The name is derived from the Latin words *nulla* (no) and *arbor* (tree).

Adelaide's eye-catching Festival Centre, home of the biennial Festival of Arts. This streamlined modern building has been acclaimed by international critics as the finest performing venue in the world.

Stark white twin ghost gums stand sentinel over the spectacular MacDonnell Ranges near Alice Springs in the Northern Territory.

(Right)
The Warrumbungle National Park contains some of the most spectacular scenery in Australia. Warrumbungle is the Aboriginal word for 'broken mountains'.

Emus stalk majestically across the inland plains and open forest country of the continent. The emu's image appears with that of the kangaroo on the Australian Coat of Arms.

Sun sets over the skeletal limbs of drowned trees in the Murray River near Berri in South Australia.

Lush shallow lagoons and billabongs in Kakadu National Park in the Northern Territory attract thousands of waterbirds.

(Previous pages)

A welcome oasis at Birdsville, the most isolated settlement in Queensland.

Ordered vineyards stretch across the Hunter Valley in New South Wales—one of the most important wine-growing districts in Australia.

Rugged Bluff Knoll in the Stirling Ranges, Western Australia.

There is more action underground at Coober Pedy than above.
Hundreds of opal mines have been excavated and most of the
population lives underground to escape the severe temperatures,
often reaching 54°C.

The attire of the Surfers Paradise meter maids attempts to soften the blow of a parking ticket in this holiday resort.

(Left)

One of the most familiar sounds of the Australian bush is the raucous laughter of the friendly kookaburra, a member of the kingfisher family.

Crystal-clear, deep blue waters of the Victoria River in the Northern Territory reflect the glowing ochre rock walls of the tree-lined gorges.

(Following page)

Sunlight highlights the Cazneaux Tree at Wilpena in the Flinders Ranges, South Australia. This tree was first photographed in 1937 by famous Australian photographer Harold Cazneaux.

Acknowledgements

The publishers wish to acknowledge the valuable assistance of the Australian Picture Library staff and the people whose material is held by the Australian Picture Library.

Australian Picture Library / VOLVOX: pages 13, 23 (above left)

Australian Picture Library/ZEFA: pages 19 (below), 34 (below right)

Robert Armstrong: page 19 (above right)

Douglass Baglin: pages 21 (above left), 29 (below)

John Baker: pages 27 (above), 32 (above), 39 (above right), 45 (above left), 46 (above right), 50 (below), 54 (below right)

John Carnemolla: front cover (main photograph), pages 4, 8 (below left), 10–11, 12 (above left, and below), 14 (below), 15 (above and below), 16 (above and below right), 18, 20 (below), 22, 23 (above right), 26 (bottom), 27 (below left), 28, 29 (above), 32 (below left and right), 34 (below left), 35 (above right, and below), 36 (above and below), 39 (above left), 40–1, 43 (below), 45 (above right), 48 (above), 51, 52–3, 54 (above), 56–7, 58, 59 (below), 61 (left)

Dive 2000: pages 23 (below), 38 (below)

Ron Dorman: pages 24–5, 55

D. & J. Heaton: front cover (inset), back cover, pages 2–3, 8 (below right), 26 (centre), 43 (above)

L. & B. Hemmings: pages 14 (above), 42 (below right), 47

Owen Hughes: pages 20 (above), 21 (below)

Roderick Hulsbergen: pages 45 (below left)

Tony Joyce: page 44 (above)

Noeline Kelly: pages 19 (above left), 44 (below), 45 (below right), 46 (above left), 48 (below), 49, 50 (above left), 51 (above), 61 (right)

Gary Lewis: pages 7, 8 (above), 27 (below right), 37, 62

Middenway & Jones: page 33 (above)

Herb Parkin: pages 6, 26 (top left), 33 (below), 59 (above)

Fritz Prenzel: pages 5, 9, 21 (above right), 30–1, 35 (above left), 39 (below), 60

Derek Roff: pages 26 (top right), 38 (above left), 54 (below left)

Brian Scott: page 12 (above right)

Paul Steel: pages 17 (below), 34 (above), 38 (above right), 42 (above and below left)

Wes Thompson: pages 16 (below left), 46 (below)

Steve Vidler: pages 17 (above), 50 (above right)

Index